Orc

Care

*Growing Orchids
Flowers and Orchids
Plants the Easy Way*

Table of Contents

Introduction

Orchids are one of the largest families in the Plant Kingdom and there are more than 30,000 known species all over the world but biologists are still discovering new varieties. Most orchids prefer to live in warm weather thus they are abundant in the tropical regions. However, there are some species of orchids that have been discovered in altitudes from 800 to 2,000 meters above sea level and there have also been varieties discovered in the Arctic Circle.

Growing orchids is a fun hobby and many people want to grow orchids because these plants are very beautiful and the hobby can be turned into a lucrative enterprise for many serious hobbyists. Contrary to popular belief, orchid care is not really difficult at all. If you are planning to grow orchids in your place, then this book will serve as your guide to growing and caring for orchids.

Chapter 1: Understanding Orchid Basics

Orchids are divided into three categories which include land types, epiphytes and lithophytes. Land types are rooted on the soil while epiphytes have roots that attach to trees while lithophytes are orchids that fasten themselves to rocks in order to develop. Out of the three categories, the epiphytes are the most abundant. This chapter will discuss about important information about orchids.

Orchid Morphology

Orchids can easily be distinguished from other plants as they display evident differences from your usual land plants.   This section will discuss about orchid morphology which refers to the structures of orchid plants that make them truly unique.

Stems

Orchids lack a permanent woody structure and they can grow in either monopodial or sympodial patterns.

The former pattern refers to the stem growing from a single bud and the leaves are added from the apex thus the stem grows longer. Orchids growing in monopodial pattern often grow several meters in length. The latter pattern, on the other hand, refers to the growth of adjacent shoots that replace old growth. Orchids with this type of growth pattern grow vertically.

Roots

Orchids often have different types of roots depending on which habitat they are found. For instance, terrestrial orchids have corms or tubers that allow them to survive during harsh winter periods as well as proliferate on land. On the other hand, epiphytic orchids or those that thrive on trees need specialized roots that allow them to fasten themselves to tree trunks. The aerial roots are made from modified spongy epidermis that efficiently collects water from humidity.

Leaves

Orchids are monocots thus they have simple leaves with parallel veins. The leaves may take form of the shape of lanceolate, ovate and orbiculate that is fibrous to prevent them from losing too much water. It is interesting to take note that most orchid leaves are perennial which means that they can live for several years before the plant sheds them off. On the other hand, there are some orchid species that lack leaves and, instead, rely on their green roots to photosynthesize or harvest sugars from tree trunks from which they are fastened to.

Flowers

There are many structural variations of the flowers of orchids and this is the reason why many people turn into orchid collectors. Some orchids may have single flowers but most have a large number of flowers. The flowers usually stem from the basal or the apex depending on the species. Although orchid flowers have different structural variations, they have almost the same components of other plant families. However the difference is that the pollen is released as single grains and is held together by a glue-like substance so that it sticks easily to the body of the pollinators.

Fruits And Seeds

Orchids are flowering plants so naturally they produce fruits and seeds. Once fertilized, the ovary develops into a capsule that remains closed at both ends. The seeds are microscopic and also very abundant inside the seed pod and once the fruit ripens, it breaks open and blows off the seeds just like spores. Unfortunately, germinating orchids from seeds is more challenging than other plant families. The thing is that all orchid species are mycoheterotrophic during germination which means that it relies on several fungi in order to germinate and complete their life cycles.

Orchid Reproduction

There are two ways for orchids to reproduce and these include cross pollination and asexual reproduction. This section will discuss orchid reproduction so that you will have an idea on how to produce more orchids on your own.

Cross Pollination

Orchids have specialized pollination systems thus orchid flowers are very receptive for long periods. Orchids have highly colorful flowers that make pollinators visually attracted to them. However, there are some orchids that emit special compounds that attract insects to pollinate them. Such compounds include zingerone, raspberry ketone and methyl eugenol. Once there is successful pollination, the petals and sepals wilt but they still remain attach to the ovary to become parts of the forming fruits.

Asexual Reproduction

Some species of orchids are also capable of asexual reproduction. For instance, orchids from the genus *Vanda, Dendrobium* and *Phalaenopsis* produce plantlets or offshoots from the nodes of the stem. This happens when the stem accumulates growth hormones to encourage shoots from growing.

Uses Of Orchids

Orchids are mainly grown for their appeal and aesthetics. However, there are some orchids that are grown for economic purposes. For instance, the orchid *Vanilla planifolia* is grown for its pods which are the source of the highly prized spice vanilla. Moreover, orchids are also used in different regions for medical purposes. For instance, the starch tubers of some orchids are used in Turkey to create concoctions that can heal colds, diarrhea and other ailments. Orchids are also used to make cosmetics. For instance, the flowers of *Orchis mascula* and *Cymbidium grandiflorum* are used for their moisturizing and restorative properties.

Chapter 2: Basic Care For Orchids

Taking care of orchids is not really difficult. In fact, orchids are considered as one of the sturdiest plants that you can grow. If this is your first time growing orchids, then do not fret. This chapter will serve as your in-depth guide on how to grow and care for your orchids.

Environmental Parameters For Successful Growth

Successfully growing your own orchids requires important growth parameters. Orchids are like other plants and they require different elements in order to thrive well. This section will discuss about the different physical parameters that your plants need in order to grow.

Light

Light is an important factor to the successful development of orchids. Most orchids need a lot of light but they do not tolerate direct sunlight. The thing is that orchids do not receive direct sunlight in the wild because light is filtered by the canopy of trees. If you are growing orchids inside the house, place them in a location near windows so that they can get the light that they need to grow. On the other hand, you can install special artificial lighting to your plants if you don't have enough natural light. Light is very important because the lack of it causes the orchids to have brittle stems, yellowing of leaves and the inability of the plant to produce flowers.

Water

Water is very important when growing orchids. Orchids require water in order to stay hydrated and nourished. Water makes it easy for the nutrients to become available to orchids. However, watering your orchid does not necessarily mean putting water any time of the day. Orchids are quite sensitive when it comes to the type of water that you use to feed them. Below are the tips on how to water your orchids.

- Do not water your orchids with the first water from your tap at your disposal. Tap water has very high hardness, pH level, chlorine and other components that can damage the roots of your plants. Take note that orchids, in their natural habitat, use water that are soft and are free from additives.

- Water the plants with water low in mineral salts like sodium and calcium. You can use bottled waters to water your plant or you can install a water filtration system if you have many plants in your house. By using a water filtration system, you can also ensure that the pH levels, hardness and mineral content of your water are kept at minimum or zero.

- When it comes to the frequency of watering, make sure that you adjust it according to the temperature conditions. For instance, you may need to water more often during summer and less during winter season.

- Make sure that the substrate of your orchid is partially dry between watering or before you water it again. Overwatering your orchids can kill them easily. The problem is not necessarily the amount of water that gets absorbed by the orchid but the availability of moisture encourages the growth of bacteria which can infect the roots and stems of the orchids. Thus

15

if you notice the swamping in your substrate, improve the drainage of your orchid to prevent damaging the roots.

- To improve the drainage of your orchids, you can pace the pot where they are planted on top a container with clay pellets to drain the plants well. You can also dip the pot to a container that is filled with water without the water getting to the top of the pot. Leave the plants about 10 minutes to absorb the water that it needs and drain well.

- Orchids that do not have any pseudobulbs (particularly those that are epiphytic) are susceptible to dehydration thus they require frequent watering than other species of orchids.

Nutrients

Orchids also require the right nutrients in order to grow well. However, unlike other plant families, orchids require different blends of fertilizers. This means that you cannot use the usual fertilizers that you apply on your other plants to nourish your orchids.

There are two methods to provide nutrients to your orchids. One of the methods is to dissolve fertilizers on irrigation water and applying it directly while watering the plant. Another method is to apply foliar fertilizers which are fertilizers applied directly to the leaves of the plants. The two methods are very effective as orchids can absorb nutrients from both roots and leaves. Below are the things that you need to consider when fertilizing your orchids.

- **Use good orchid quality fertilizers.** There are many opinions regarding which fertilizer is the best for your orchids and even if this is the case, it is important that you take note that you need a fertilizer that contains three major elements for the growth of your orchids which are nitrogen, phosphorus and potassium. It is also important that your fertilizer contains traces of sulfur, magnesium, calcium, iron, boron, manganese, zinc and molybdenum. Moreover, it is crucial to choose low-urea or urea-free fertilizers especially if you are growing epiphytic orchids because urea is not a source of nitrogen for epiphytes.

- **Water weekly but weekly.** This is an old rule of thumb every orchid gardener must know.

Orchids do not need to be fed all the time thus it is important that you apply only tiny amounts of fertilizers to your plants to prevent overwhelming them. Overfeeding your plant is not a good thing especially if you use synthetic fertilizers. Such fertilizers contain mineral salts which can build up in your pot overtime which eventually damages your plants. So instead of making your plants healthy, overfeeding kills them.

- **Fertilize only during growing season.** Many orchids go to dormancy during the winter months and the best thing to break the dormancy is to fertilize them. The thing is that plants, when they start to show fresh growth during spring, are deprived from nutrients for a long time thus it is important to fertilize them.

- **Use the right blend of fertilizers.** To encourage the plants to flower, you need to decrease the amount of phosphorus and nitrogen that you feed to your plat and increase the potassium. Having said this, you need to use the right blend of fertilizers if you want to achieve the right growth of your plants.

Temperature

Temperature is an important parameter to ensure that successful growth of your orchids. The thing is that different species of orchids are distributed in different climates all over the world but most are found in the tropical regions thus they require warmer temperatures. Common families of orchids like Cymbidium, Cattleya, Phalaenopsis and Vandas to name a few require a minimum temperature of no less than 9 °C and should not exceed 30 °C. Orchids cannot withstand higher temperature because an increase in the temperature can often lead to dehydration in your orchids.

If you live in the sub tropics, then growing orchids outside should not be a problem for you unless you experience frost. However, growing tropical orchids might present a huge challenge if you are in the temperate regions. Having said this, growing orchids indoors is a great option for you to successfully propagate orchids.

Humidity

Humidity is an important environmental factor for growing orchids successfully. Although important, it is also considered as the most difficult to control. Most orchids, in their natural habitat, require a relative humidity of 40% but this is not often followed if the plants are already grown away from their habitat. Below is a table to show the different humidity requirements of common species of orchids.

Orchid Genus	Humidity
Cattleya	50 - 80%
Miltonia	70% and below
Vanda	80%
Epidendrum	20 - 60%
Paphiopedilium	40 - 50%
Dendrobidium	20 - 60%
Oncidium	20 - 60%
Cymbidium	40 - 60%
Phalaenopsis	50 - 80%

Different genus of orchids requires different levels of relative humidity. New gardeners would be better off choosing plants that do not require high relative humidity such as Oncidiums and Dendrobiums. However, if you still want to enjoy caring for orchids that require high relative humidity, below are the strategies on how you can improve the humidity for your orchids without installing any high-end devices.

- Group all your orchids in a single area to create a microclimate. The thing is that orchids, just like other plants, transpire and if they are grouped together, they create humidity thus making it easier for them to autonomously maintain the moisture level. You can place the plants in a stepped way or in a tier to create a cascade of air flow within. This arrangement is also necessary so that the moisture given off by the plants at the lowest tier is used by those in the upper tier.

- Place several clay pellets at the base of your pots to hold water. Make sure that the water does not get in contact with the roots to avoid the development of root rot. The water under the clay pellets provide moisture to maintain the desired relative humidity that your orchid requires.

- Installing a fountain with moving water near your orchids is a great way to maintain humidity. Now you know why orchid greenhouses often add a cascading waterfall. It is not only to add beauty to your orchid garden but also maintain the moisture level. Now if you only have a side table as your "orchid garden", you can buy a miniature water fall and it works just the same as a cascading water fall.

- If you live near a body of water – whether a sea or a river, you can provide moisture to your orchids by opening your windows temporarily.

- You can also use hand vaporizers to provide moisture if you only have a few orchids in your house. The problem, however, you need to spritz your orchids several times during the day especially if the weather gets very hot.

- If you have enough budget, you can buy an electronic humidifier. The best thing about an electric humidifier is that you can predetermine the moisture level in the setting and also use a timer to make the humidifier work only at certain times during the day.

Ventilation

Orchids do not thrive well in environments with little Oxygen. In fact, if methane sources are close such as decaying organic matter are present, it inhibits the flowering of most orchid species. To ensure that your orchids survive, you need to proper ventilation all throughout the day but avoid direct air currents on your plants.

Maintaining proper ventilation can be very tricky. The thing is that if you provide too much air on your orchids, the humidity might drop which can cause your plants to become dehydrated. Having said this, there should be a balance between ventilation and other environmental factors such as moisture.

However, if you don't ventilate well, it can result to the buildup of high levels of humidity as well as temperature that can promote the growth of bacteria, viruses and fungi that can greatly affect your orchid's health. For safe measures, make sure that you provide proper ventilation to your orchids by opening a window at certain times of the day.

Grooming Your Orchids

It is important that you properly groom your orchids for many various reasons. Grooming is a way to train your orchids to grow in a structure that you want as well as prevent the plants from easily getting infected by diseases and pests. This section will discuss about the many ways on how you can groom your orchids.

- **Cut the rods.** Groom your orchids by cutting the flower stem once it has lost all of its flowers. By cutting the flower stem, this also encourages the formation of "keiki" which is the new flower sucker of the orchid.

- **Separate infected plant from the rest of your healthy orchids.** By quarantining the infected plant, you prevent the different types of diseases to spread to your remaining healthy plants. Apply the necessary treatments to your infected plants and reintroduce them to the healthy plants.

- **Remove the organic materials at the base of the orchids.** Periodically, dead leaves and fallen flowers might be collected at the bottom. The dead materials can be source of diseases such as fungi and insects.

Choosing Containers For Your Orchids

Orchids can be planted in different containers but just because you can plant them in containers does not mean that you can already plant them on any container that you want. It is important to take note that different types of orchids require different types of pots. Below are the different types of pots that you can use for your orchids.

- **Plastic pots.** Plastic pots are lightweight and they come with several drainage holes. Plastic pots are inert and are not a good conductor of heat thus the medium tends to dry out slower than clay pots. When choosing plastic pots, opt for those that have thick walls and do not break easily. You can also choose clear polyethylene pots to make sure that the light reaches to the roots. This is especially true if you are growing orchids that photosynthesize through their roots.

- **Terra cotta pots.** Terra cotta pots are made from clay and they are heavier thus more stable. This type of pot is great for growing orchids outdoors because they cannot be easily toppled down by strong winds. Cymbidia grows well if planted in terra cotta pots.

- **Basket pots.** Orchids that have pendant flowers or are heavy rooted are better off planted in basket pots. Basket pots are usually made from different materials like plastic, wire, wood and mesh. The advantage of basket pots is that they allow the air to circulate around the roots.

When planting orchids on pots, make sure that you provide support to your plant by putting in the right substrate. Moreover, do not fret if your orchids have extensive root systems after being planted in a pot for a long time. You might think that it is time to repot them but the thing it is the roots that provide them nourishment so you don't need to repot them all too soon.

Choosing The Right Substrate For Your Orchids

There are different types of substrate that you can use for your orchids. Although there are different types of substrates for your orchids, what you need to do is to choose those that drain well. Most orchids bought at garden centers are usually epiphytes thus they need light as well as porous soil. Below are the types of substrates that you can use to grow your orchids.

Type of potting mix	Advantages	Disadvantages
Expanded clay aggregate (Aliflor)	Provides proper aeration Does not decompose	It is a heavy type of potting mix
Coconut husk chunks	Retains moisture Provides proper aeration Slowly decomposes	Needs to be cleaned properly to remove salt residue May retain too much moisture
Coconut husk fiber	Retains water well Slowly decomposes	Does not drain well unlike coconut husk chunks
Gravel	Drains well Very inexpensive	Heavy Nutrient deficient
Fir bark	Accessible Inexpensive Available in many sizes Lightweight	Can be difficult to wet Easily decomposes
Hardwood charcoal	Slowly decomposes Efficient in absorbing contaminants	Holds very little amount of moisture Can produce a lot of dust when dry

Lava rock	Drains well Does not decompose	Very heavy
Perlite	Very lightweight Provides proper aeration Has good water retention Very cheap	Retains a lot of water
Sphagnum moss	Retains water Provides good aeration Is very accessible	Retain too much water if packed tightly
Styrofoam	Accessible Inexpensive Well-draining	Should not be used alone because it does not retain water or other nutrients
Tree fern fiber	Slowly decomposes Rapidly draining	Very expensive Has low water retention

Orchids are very easy to grow and it is important that you only use the recommended soils mentioned in this section. Never use soil that you grow your vegetables in otherwise it will drown the roots of your orchids.

Chapter 3: Troubleshooting Orchid Problems

Orchids are hardy plants but this does not mean that they are invincible to problems. This chapter will discuss about the different type of troubleshooting tips and tricks to grow healthy orchids in your home.

Indicators Of Orchid Problems

You know that your orchid is in trouble by looking at the state of the plant's roots and leaves. This section will discuss about the indicators of orchid problems so that you will be able to implement solutions to the problem.

Roots

One of the evidences that are conclusive to the good health of your orchids is the status of the roots. Roots that are hydrated and healthy appear green while dried roots appear white. So if you notice that most of your roots are white, then you need to water them regularly until they turn green in a few days.

Leaves

It is also important that you look periodically at the condition of the leaves to know if your orchids are suffering from problems. Orchid leaves are naturally green but if you notice a brownish tinge of the leaves, this is a clear indicator that the orchid is receiving excess light than needed. However, if the leaves are yellowish, then it is a clear indication that it is receiving less light ach day. Another thing to check on the leaves is the texture. Leaves that are fleshy are indicative of a healthy plant while leaves that are weak indicate lack of moisture. On the other hand, the state of the leaves also indicate if your orchids are being attacked by different diseases.

Orchid Diseases

Orchids suffer from different diseases caused by fungi, bacteria, virus and insect pests. If you want to grow orchids successfully, then it is crucial that you know how to detect these diseases and also provide possible solution to the problem. This section will discuss about the different types of orchid diseases you ought to know.

Fungi

Fungal infection greatly affects most species of orchids. They are usually present as dark spots on the leaves as well as on the flowers. The presence of fungal infection can also cause the color of the leaves to change from green to yellow or black depending on the gravity of the infection. The culprit behind fungal infection on orchids is the presence of excessive moisture, high temperatures and poor ventilation. The best thing to do to prevent fungi diseases is to control the environmental conditions. Applying the right fungicide can also help prevent the spread of the disease to other healthy plants.

Bacteria

Orchids are also receptive towards bacterial infection. It causes spots on the leaves as well as on the pseudobulbs. Bacterial infections on orchids are often very aggressive and it can lead to the death of the plant quickly. The proliferation of harmful bacteria on the orchids is usually facilitated by high humidity. If your plant is infected with bacteria, the best thing to do is to cut off the affected part and isolate the plant. Avoid watering the plant to prevent the bacteria from proliferating. Unfortunately, there is no effective way to treat bacterial infection in orchids but you can always disinfect your orchids with powdered cinnamon because it has antibacterial properties and does not have any adverse side effects on the plants.

Virus

Virus also presents another problem to orchids. When virus attacks orchids, it causes a wide variety of symptoms. The most common symptoms include dark spots or dots appearing on the leaves. The leaf can also turn black from the margins. Other symptoms include yellowing of the leaves and malformation or stunting of the leaves as well as the flowers. Removal of the infected part is very important to control the progression of the disease.

Pests

Pest infestation is a normal problem in orchids. Insects often live on plants for nutrients but the problem becomes adverse if the plant is on compromised health. The most common insect pest of orchids is aphids which suck the sap from the orchids which often results to the stunting of the plant. Other parasites that affect the plants include mealy bugs, mites, sappers and even caterpillars that feed on the leaves. The basic treatment for insect infestation is to apply insecticides and acaricides. But if you are concerned about using dangerous synthetic pesticides, you can always use organic pesticides to rid your orchids from pets. Now if the pest has caused a lot of damage to the plant, you can cut off the affected area instead.

Common Solutions To Orchid Problems

Troubleshooting orchid problems can be a daunting task especially to first timers. This section will provide a list of the anomalous problems of orchid plants, their effects as well as possible solutions. This will serve as an easy reference guide to all orchid enthusiasts.

Condition	Effects	Solutions
Inadequate lighting	Flowering is hampered. Weak stems develop and the plant loses vigor.	Relocate your orchids so that they receive enough light. If you cannot find a good location, supplement by using artificial lights.
Inadequate humidity	The leaves shrivel and appear weak. The plants, if already flowering, stop developing the buds. The roots will appear very white and dry and the leaves will eventually turn yellow and will fall.	Water more often or install a humidifier to control the humidity on your plants.
Temperatures too hot or too cold	Excess or absence of eat can produce the flowers to fall off.	Relocate the plant to a place where there is optimal temperature for proper growth.
Too much irrigation	The roots easily rot and adapt a flimsy texture. The leaves turn yellow and the	Do not overwater your orchids. Wait for the soil to turn dry before you water. If

	plants eventually die.	the roots have already begun to rot, remove the affected part and transplant the healthy plant to another pot.
Leaves get burned from the sun	The leaves appear to have burns or take the yellow color.	Relocate to an area where the orchid receives only adequate lighting. Filter the light by putting them inside a greenhouse.
Too much fertilizers	The edges of the leaves turn yellow.	Do not fertilize your plants. Avoid using hard water which can also be a source of trace elements.
Presence of organic gases like methane	If your orchids are planted near a compost bin, it often displays premature falling off of flowers and wilting of leaves.	Relocate the orchids to an area where there is minimal presence of organic gases. Provide proper aeration.
Pollinating insects	Pollinating insects are not really a threat to your orchids but since	Protect your plants from insect pollinators by putting

	orchids are grown for their flowers, pollination through insects means subsequent closure of the plants once it is fertilized. It simply shortens the life of the flower	them in an enclosed screen. Do not use pesticides because insect pollinators are useful.
Draught	Too much draught can cause premature dropping of the flowers.	Provide proper ventilation.

Other Tips To Make Orchids Healthy

Ensuring the success of your orchids require you to have good cultural practices. Below are other helpful tips that you need to do to make sure that your orchids are healthy.

- When you manipulate or groom your orchids, make sure that you work with clean hands or gloves. This is to prevent the spread of diseases.

- Disinfect your tools before cutting some parts of your orchids. You can disinfect by soaking the tools to a mixture of bleach and water.
- If you cut a plant part, make sure that you disinfect the wound left by the cut. Use cinnamon powder and dust the wound of the plant.

Conclusion

Orchids are prized for their beautiful flowers and the only way to grow such beauties is to make sure that the entire plant is healthy. Caring for orchids is not really that complicated and even beginners can have success in their endeavors as long as they have the right guide on how to go about with the right practices. Let this book serve as your guide on how to grow such beautiful plants to improve your house as well as your garden.

Printed in Great Britain
by Amazon